KIM KARDASHIAN'S MARRIAGE

by the same author

81 AUSTERITIES

SAM RIVIERE

Kim Kardashian's Marriage

FABER & FABER

First published in 2015
by Faber & Faber Ltd
Bloomsbury House
74–77 Great Russell Street
London WC1B 3DA

Typeset by Hamish Ironside
Printed in Great Britain by Martins the Printers

The right of Sam Riviere to be identified as author of this work
has been asserted in accordance with Section 77 of the Copyright,
Designs and Patents Act 1988

Some of these poems appeared in *I Love Roses When They're Past Their
Best*, *The Lifeboat*, *Pleiades*, *Test Centre Four* and *The Harlequin*

A CIP record for this book is available from the British Library

ISBN 978-0-571-32143-8

6 8 10 9 7

Contents

I want that forever love
KIM KARDASHIAN, 2012

[PRIMER]

spooky berries

Edgar Allan Poe
has written a very eerie poem this month
with many allusions to the latest botanical blogging.

A very cute hand
carved natural pumpkin
hanging about 6.5 ft in the air,

and my little lens wasn't cutting it.
So I popped on my big lens
and got it all.

thirty-three dust

Dark shadows melded with the night sky,
making it difficult to tell
where the land met the heavens.

Egypt. This rigid regime.
Black & white photos, zonal winds.
The three most dusty summers.

The inventor of rock & roll, among others,
allowed to dry in a gentle stream of clean air,
then stored in a dust-proof container.

american sunglasses

In the movie *The American*
(the 2010 film *The American*,
which sees George Clooney
as Jack, an assassin and gunsmith) George Clooney
(looking effortless in the Persol
3009) wears a pair of Havana-coloured Persol
2883 sunglasses.

ice-cream hardcore

I dreamt about chasing down an ice-cream truck,
and then finding an ice-cream truck parked.

Ordered the pineapple ice-cream.

infinity weather

Godfather of clocks,
defy weather and waves,
set for colonisation of moon.

Give me one minute,
I'll give you cosmic.

beautiful pool

The splendour of Florida's Gulf Coast
is rivalled by the elegant interior
of your luxurious two bedrooms.

Do you have a dream to build?
This image is minimalist.
Beautiful green grass scattered on the ground.

I really surprised myself
with several patios and intricate corridors,
antiques saved from around the world.

Like, I mean I knew I was that good.
I just didn't think I could do it
under that much pressure.

View images as a 'river of photos',
immaculate and perfect.

the new sunsets

What's life really like
in an active-adult retirement community?

Sunset thru the trees.
It's always beautiful.

Thanks for sharing.

girlfriend sincerity

It is best to keep the letter simple and brief.
You really have to feel what you're saying.
When you talk to her, be honest,

and entertaining when you run.
Make her feel like a sexual object.
Express how you appreciate her

breaking up with you. If you are truly
inside your efforts then who understands?
I'm still   the main issue here

is commitment. Here are 25 sweet things.

grave heaven

All our emotions, thoughts,
knowledge and feelings go to an eccentric,
swashbuckling fantasy world.

Or am I missing something?

Do good people really go
to an anime-inspired fantasy world
when they die?

[CONTOUR]

american dust

A supernova that went off in 1987
produced large quantities of dust,
which may explain why galaxies
in the early universe were so dusty.

I DO NOT OWN OR TAKE CREDIT
FOR THIS SONG.
Format: Cassette, Limited Edition, C60.
Country: USA.

ice-cream sunglasses

One night we were speeding forward
like the fire cornered

behind the balloons & sunglasses
that show palm trees in the lenses.

Jo's soft as ice-cream though,
so stare away.

infinity hardcore

This has been a huge trend.

But it ain't enough.

How much remixes can you make.

Oooooooohh! Oooooooohh!

This one's for you.

beautiful weather

The television weathercasters
are becoming more and more stunning
and beautiful over the years,
and some have attracted more viewers
than Bill's 'perfect' English.

This song is for Billy Clyde Tuggle.
I hope you make it to Tahiti.

the new pool

Summer is here. The glorious season
of the year when most of us
take life a little less seriously.

Most folks will only need one chemical.
You may not win,
but at least you won't look like a jerk.

Live tour should go back to how it was,
the new system is crap go back
to the old system.

girlfriend sunsets

Melodic death metal, black metal,
death metal folk and Viking metal.

29 years old.
Let's be honest guys.

Basically you charter a catamaran
and propose to your girlfriend.

grave sincerity

When will disreputable nihilism become boring?
Hopefully never. They flatter with their tongue.

What explanation can you offer to me for pretending
in matters of importance style is the vital thing?

Grave sincerity lacks greyness, means dead serious.
This seems to be all anyone can talk about today.

spooky heaven

Sounds like heaven
remixed for my Halloween party.

thirty-three berries

It took some gentle prodding by my part,
placing a plump blueberry in her palm
and telling her to take her time.

Another name for the sweet purple-red
morphed into a multi-faceted, holistic
marketing communications firm with offices.

Indeed.
My fishing life began thirty-three years ago,
in the company of cousin Ricky.

[HIGHLIGHT]

infinity sunglasses

A comprehensive selection
hidden in the high-rise.

You know what this means?!
eyes love infinity

fucking pimped out
FREE SHIPPING

beautiful hardcore

Remove her clothes and naked.
Sleep on bed in boys.
Mandy, SophieCindy, Muzika, Igri, Chalga, Bezplatno,
    Mandy –

for all things sexy and beautiful
those that are hot and dirty
everything hardcore and raw

if it were all wrapped up in a box and sent to you
that box would read . . .
Beautiful Pornstar Cleopatra Hardcore Orgy.

the new weather

This radar loop is delayed and downsized.

Long-range forecast through the looking glass.

Tornados, wildfires, droughts and floods

were once seen as disasters striking the brain.

Also mentioned: what I felt was the most

interesting theme of the conference:

that of freak conditions.

girlfriend pool

She wanted to go for a swim
even though I said
it was going to be cold.

I was at a cottage.
I spied on my sister
and her girlfriend tanning

after running
last summer.
HOLY MOLY.

A few condoms,
a few minor mental issues
courtesy of the weirdos.

We're glad you asked.
It's a way of hanging.

grave sunsets

I said to her, now that is to my liking,
as clouds sail by golden-red,
aided by smoke from fuel-reduction burns
in the nearby forests.

From the first breath that you take
I'll be there for you.
We'll laugh until we have to cry.
I am familiar with the scenario,

the last home
of Hollywood icon Marilyn Monroe
and with their interpretation of the word.
Three days in the grave.

I don't wanna feel the emptiness.

spooky sincerity

a salesperson
corny:
lacking new ideas
unpleasant and sometimes rude

who used to delve
into this unique entertainment industry
by paying homage
to strange and frightening experiences

in bonus footage
from the documentary film
that continues to compel
spellbinds

by virtue of sheer incongruity
& absence of commitment
creepy big pink
hair celebrity

autograph famous
kiss lipstick video
might be the funniest yet
left a splodge of blood on the bedspread

an invaluable resource
for non-native English speakers, that is

thirty-three heaven

I pay homage to this world,
and to the master,
a horse from heaven.

american berries

Various dark-fruited, as distinguished from blue-fruited,
essays, novels and poems give voice to a provocative
but consistent portrait of a Native American.
Profound and honest thinkers, edible
in fall, perfect for making jellies.
Definition: Cute Killers.

ice-cream dust

With a blazing disappointing summer
Jenkins returned to his solo work.
Surely we are thinking
lavender barbecues
a mint leaf
briefly reunited
with a little more honey,
so many that I could taste the egginess.

[POWDER]

the new hardcore

This is an all-out onslaught
that very much lives up to the tech spec.

Special edition 2.0 appears on the web.
But is it a fake?

I'm starting a band
about the negative fan reaction

to November.
Over half are women aged 25–44.

Can someone recommend me
more women.

I'm slowly getting into
associated subculture.

girlfriend weather

A lot of guys
particularly the nerdy
wish to uncover
very good men's fashion advice,

also to wear clothes
based on your girlfriend's dad.
Trust you to confuse whether she virgin or not.

You might ease tension by talking,
make use of the hot weather.
She is a real problem.

grave pool

The president lay a wreath.
Pool was not able to see this
cemetery scene, but
the upper river is shallow.
Much of its relaxing greenery
comes in a little glass vial.

Sun deck, central lily pads,
stones (one for his own
windswept landscape);
'black marble' was noted,
and his brother Edmond's
sculpture of the morning.

spooky sunsets

I took these pictures with a 30-sec. exposure
and a high ISO setting of 1600
to enhance the look of dark days,
an ominous, solid mantle of clouds
with just a sliver of bright sky streaking through.

Are you brave enough for our very final finale?
I have a cat, I have a band or two.
We've got cocktails for grown-ups.

I used to review every movie I watched.

thirty-three sincerity

Concerning the stupidity of evil,
commercial culture:
thirty-three poems.

Mary J. Blige:
twenty-two additional poems,
'the second of four children'.

A recapitulation of the formulation
of the aesthetic conflict:
fifty-two poems,

and a reformulation:
the fragrance's unprecedented success
broke sales records in hours.

At fifteen my heart was set on candour,
at thirty I stood learning
modern lyric poetry,

funeral prayer
firm hypocrisy.
At forty I had no opposite.

american heaven

With its super-size skyline and facsimile architecture
the level of heaven we develop within us
is the level it was possible to imagine
of the assorted early 80s, on earth.

God does not force anyone to heaven.
I could just leave it at that.

ice-cream berries

Texture is over.
No flavour will fool you.
I'm not talking about basketball.
I'm talking about the madness
that is a less heavy version.
In New Orleans
I'm also doing a bit of entertaining.

infinity dust

You may be wondering how I learned the title.
I'll tell you how. I have a very annoying problem.
With practised skill I play several hours
and the screen itself . . . I can't.

These versatile pieces based on a future
that has passed
introduce us to the wonders of a vision
that three dust particles are stuck between.

A newly settled moon could be used as an objective marker.
Heart keeps beating
to the base of trucks and voitures
and it is nice and everything but it's a DESIGN FLAW,

specs in the eyes of infinity.
This book has an extremely interesting afterword,
you are just evil. Make a strike
or only make greens.

beautiful sunglasses

Since I am a model I have to think a lot

      inspiring picture

for my security and protection

      we heart it

I am keen in my profession so always
want to look best and presentable

      looking for cheap we supply cheap

Actress Nicollette Sheridan was enjoying
the beautiful beaches
of Saint Barts on Christmas Day wearing
the new Christian Dior
worn by Dimitra Spanou in 'beautiful Greece'

      on background blue sky
      she looks like this and more

[BLEND]

grave weather

His wife's graveside service
was just barely finished,
when there was a massive
clap of thunder, followed
by a tremendous bolt of
lightning, accompanied by
a sunflower's pollination.

spooky pool

This peeling facade was once the grand entrance
to a long-gone attraction in what is a now a slightly
beautiful light at the end of the day, Saturday.
The lights will be dimmed for atmosphere swims.

thirty-three sunsets

Viewed from the west, the game got more physical.
Three of them, barefoot, try desperately
to capture the water, a beautiful clear blue.

They boast of a thirty-page text, and are positioned
perfectly with centred sunset. A barge-shaped
horizon made up entirely of questions

attracts the majority of visitors. Approximately
three thousand questions, some of the most beautiful
you have ever seen – beware though, serene is repeated.

It is relatively flat. Seven of the eight took the deal.

american sincerity

Let us draw near to Russia.
Let us go right into the presence of film criticism.
Let us celebrate music since 2002.
Let us give out pies and eat corn dogs.

Jump to The Sound of Young America
with its undercurrents of guilty conscience.
We have been sprinkled with sauce by radio hosts,
not with the old blood,

nor with the speech espoused to make us clean,
not old D. H. Lawrence.
But even here we suspected as much.
It's now (a satire).

Therefore keep the network peace.
Therefore label the location,
with a heart in full idea,
with hearts fully defined in American English.

ice-cream heaven

You are a waitress in an ice-cream parlour.
'The orders just get better every time!'

infinity berries

Some years ago, it was.
I just ate some of those
things that make sour
sweet and my blood
powered a plain necklace.
I am trying to locate
variety and a feeling,
it is cushiony soft,
yet it's diamond
to the touch. Talk to me
bold in the morning.
You'll love the feather
tattooed on my flower.

beautiful dust

It's amazing what he could do,
Job is the one who said from dust
I came and the Lord taketh away.
Beautiful job!! Brings tears to my eyes.

A little sleepy, shy, neurotic guy,
this probably started with
wash me and those smiley faces,
a weakness for nebulae.

Yes, the Lord giveth but he
has come a long way since then.
Reserved, faithful, melancholy,
to dust I shall return. I have.

Which is not something you get
to say every day to those
that prefer to use their disguise.
Believer, enjoy this amazing dust.

the new sunglasses

It's here that eyewear
worn by countless
has crowned
over 100 brands.
Invest in this collection.
You can view the latest
detail on the temples,
eye-wateringly bright.

girlfriend hardcore

after he found the heart
of his girl
a tape of mine
was so broken

[SHADOW]

thirty-three pool

Hi guys! Keryn and I went swimming!
The deepest indoor swimming pool in the world.
The portal is located in Brussels, Belgium.
Its maximum depth is 34.5 metres.
I tried to bring you guys in the pool with us,
but it was too dark to see or steal her tiara.
I will confirm this tomorrow!

american sunsets

We are sorry, this thriller movie is under construction.
Picture twilight in Los Angeles: the city's labyrinth
of eight-lane freeways is jammed with millions of cars.
It rises like a dream / In the fall from a feather
Trees shed all their summers / Washes away my peach

Which is your favourite?
Loading . . . Alert icon. Noam Chomsky error . . .

ice-cream sincerity

Went to the book fair again last Saturday with Mom.
These are what she bought (for herself). I thought
I'm gonna read them too once she's done.

I expected to hate it – OK, love–hate it –
but then I found myself somewhere
that feels like the best of America.

Vanilla ice-cream floats, barbershop quartet,
the surprisingly sincere doughnut.
Mmm, sacrificial . . .

infinity heaven

From childhood, we seem to nurture pictures
so much better that it isn't even fair to compare.

beautiful berries

Fun photo of Sam and Sonia
ravishing raspberries on a recent trip
well into the winter.
Pink to red-purple with a drugstore splurge,
they are available all year around.
So pretty. Perfect for a party!

But the imagery is important this morning.

the new dust

I meet Franklin Delano Roosevelt.
He's been walking for three days.
He makes necklaces of refined sugar,
human hair is toxic now.
Melted plastic in plants is okay,
leather is sugar, metal sugar,
and sometimes rope or wool.

girlfriend sunglasses

I enjoy reflections in unusual places.
This cell phone is a good choice.
Focus your attention here.

This is my girlfriend's sunglasses.
This is a view of a monorail
as she looked an endless tunnel.

If you want to have the icon with the actual,
I was waiting for my sleeping friend to return
to send emails to your 'girlfriend',

and decided just to leave the shutter open,
and the mainstream jumps into view,
wearing the popular shark-tooth necklace trend,

ironic white glasses facialized . . .
a surprise?   A picture.
My dog, go configure.

grave hardcore

THE TRUTH is fun to discover
JAPAN is a very proud environment
THE GRAVE is owned by a new generation

spooky weather

Spotted these lights as I was heading up the stairs.
It was very cold, but wasn't snowing.
This is a repost from last October.

A few weeks ago you may recall
there was a lot of speculation in the media
about the weather for winter.

Lightning and thunder can send shudders
through your spine. Late October rain.
Drizzling down. Talent that touches your heart.

Most of us in our childhood used to fear thunder,
but see now it's just a fun for me.
I have to apologise if I'm not around the next few days.

[LINER]

ice-cream sunsets

I usually don't wander from my two regular flavours,
from soft-serve in California to scooping in Washington.

Tucked in a tree-lined complex with a stunning ocean view,
I know the current owners of this place. They took over
the establishment around the time I left high school.

They used to own A Slice of Summer;
Every day is like Sundae for years to come.
Around the west there's reason for nostalgia.
Just looking through old stuff and quite liked this one.

infinity sincerity

For a guy who claims to hate cheesy stuff,
he proved true what he said before;
that for the girl he truly love,
he'll do anything possible to show.

All this while I've been loyal to LJ. Seriously,
LJ is very easy to manage. Just the html to edit,
hath thou forsaken me, that I am blind
and cannot see the simple truth

that dwells in me. They taught me how
to dodge and lie to hide my codes.
Cut and paste the here and there.
Forget what the intentions were . . .

Four brief years ago (it seems relevant)
I was a youth in college, but some of us
were looking at the Hummingbird Animal Totem.
I panicked and now I'm doing astrophysics.

beautiful heaven

We're spreading smiles every minute
with lyrics and jokes for your personal use.

O Sovereign God transcendent!
This is an excellent song.

the new berries

New-build properties for sale
in the Shoalhaven region,
a fifteenth-century half-timbered structure
in whose grounds some of the major intellectual influences

on his life and thinking
still in existence today
are located and renamed
the wrong way.

To carry out further investigations
book an appointment.
What makes you so special,
a small opportunity on Mars?

When headed over the bridge to the cinema this evening
you're likely to hate whatever you come across.
You hit the shops,
the look of your skin having a bad day.

girlfriend dust

Today on *The Artificial Girlfriend Show*
the judges are incredulous about
the creepy stalker ex who is back
with another parody,
destroying the original's innocence.

I want cute boys with new ringtones
and telephone honesty for starters.
I want auditions for the role of the black man.
A love of Tiffany won't hurt either.
Call your guitar later.

grave sunglasses

When you ride in the wave, we come back forever dazzled.

Pic taken through a pair of glasses with orange lenses.

By Waylon's grave through Dalton's orange sunglasses.

spooky hardcore

I'm making and selling exclusive beats of that genre
and more. I also make custom beats.
So we should call ourselves 'The Untouchables'.
It looked like we weren't getting hits at all.

thirty-three weather

baridi. [cold]
joto. [warm]
wingu / mawingu. [cloud / clouds]
jua. [sun]
mvua. [rain]

We believe in this valley

american pool

A sim term used to refer to unusual
varieties of people who fancy
something a little bit different to rules.

[GLOSS]

beautiful sincerity

Soft, romantic, personal details are the key.
I think that there are so many different ways
that someone can be beautiful.
The contrast between honesty and freedom
when I try to make sense of Zelo's rap.
I think for me, without offence, the press accounts
in response to the funnies is genuineness,
or Wilfred J. Funk's brand-new collection
of the ten most sincere words in English.

the new heaven

And I saw a new heaven and a new earth – such a
    heaven and earth that they
might properly be called new; such transformations,
    and such changes.
What does the Bible mean by A New Heavens And A
    New Earth?

The Bible's Prophetic Program Culminates With 'A New
    Heaven and
A New Earth'. What might this mean? What are the
    implications of this?
Does it have, The New Earth, Wikipedia, the free
    encyclopaedia?

For as the new heavens and the new earth, which I will
    make, shall remain
before me, says the LORD; so shall your descendants
    and your name remain.
What Are the New Heavens and New Earth?

What is the meaning of the expression, 'new heavens
    and new earth'?
Does it refer to the renewal of this planet, or does it
    signify heaven itself?
What are the New Heavens and the New Earth?

What are the New Heavens and the New Earth?
Will believers spend eternity on the New Earth, or in
    the New Heavens,
or both? What Will Heaven be Like? Besides receiving
    a new body,

those who enter heaven will be given a new name and
    will be incapable
of committing sin. Therefore the new heaven and the
    new earth will not
be separate from each other; the earth of the saints,
    their glorified bodies,

will be heavenly. The old world, The New Heaven and
    New Earth, Our
Final Ending in the Lord. Good article on the New
    Heaven and New Earth
and exactly what we will be getting in this new
    environment with the Lord.

This is our final ending in the Lord. Following the
    judgment of the great white
throne depicted in the closing verses of chapter 20,
    John's attention
is next directed to the The New Heaven & The New
    Earth's official profile,
including the latest music albums, songs, music videos
    and more updates.

girlfriend berries

Maybe it's the coming summer
and my overwhelming desire
for the tomatoes and peaches
I spent my partnership with Dannon picking.
As often as I got to enjoy the 'fruits'
of your labour, I'll give the rest
to my sister to surprise her,
and hope it doesn't go to waste.

grave dust

The night I got dust on my hands after dusting off my
    mother's grave
I was lent a bass guitar for a while, and noodled in 7/8.
I heard the world's sounds whilst doing one of the early
    Alchemist's quests.
Your mother plays a significant role; that she is dead
    and gone has nothing to do with it.
So I jogged along to times and phases gathered from
    mausoleums and sarcophagi.
I can concoct a thought to work in its usage. Didn't do
    anything with the results.
Too goddamn lazy to finish our page. I dislike the arts.

spooky sunglasses

I love dressing up. But sometimes cop frames
change the eyes with some sick humour.

Contacts are not designed to improve
a person's unsafe vision of a nun & man

thru a car window in a boutique 1940s photo. Read on
for some fun, or to buy the perfect pair of decorative eyes.

thirty-three hardcore

I was led to believe but now I know for sure
there are two bands called 'Lost Freighter':
a melodic metalcore-style band from Troy,
and a dilapidated distortion machine tribute.
By the way that famous dude was racist,
like 1800s Wolfgang L. Mclain. Absolutely.
People who like Disney are a disease.

american weather

A cold rain fell across Arkansas on Friday,
washing away some of the Christmas ice and snow
that knocked out power to 194,000 customers,
making America extreme and more disaster-prone,
including the diverse serving of amateur grains:
the corn and soybean industry futures rebound.
South America is hotter, and drier-eyed.

ice-cream pool

I don't see any value in trying to promote a fake happiness
which is what I see most of the time,
putting on blinders is worse. Every parent
wants images for her child's birthday,
water fireworks & 200 pounds of dry ice.
This Thai kid is probably happier, agreed.

infinity sunsets

You have stalked this blog,
you must really like me.
Message me anytime
even if it's just to talk.
I blog about whatever I want.

Index

Index of titles

book is for Sophie